T0016176

WICCAN
TEAS &
BREWS

WICCAN TEAS & BREWS

Recipes for magical drinks, essences, and tinctures

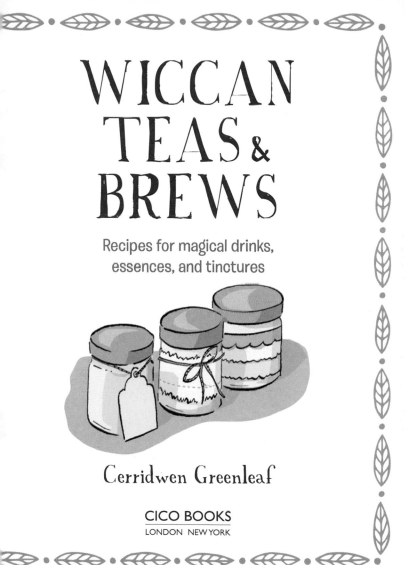

Cerridwen Greenleaf

CICO BOOKS
LONDON NEW YORK

Published in 2023 by CICO Books
An imprint of Ryland Peters & Small Ltd
20–21 Jockey's Fields   341 E 116th St
London WC1R 4BW   New York, NY 10029

www.rylandpeters.com

10 9 8 7 6 5 4 3 2 1

Text in this book originally featured in *The Book of Kitchen Witchery,*
The Magical Home, 5-minute Magic for Modern Wiccans,
The Book of Witchy Wellbeing, and *Spells for Peace of Mind.*

Text © Brenda Knight 2023
Design and illustration © CICO Books 2023

A CIP catalog record for this book is available from the
Library of Congress and the British Library.

ISBN: 978-1-80065-200-2

Printed in China

Senior Designer: Emily Breen
Illustrator: Michael Hill

Commissioning editor: Kristine Pidkameny
Art director: Sally Powell
Creative director: Leslie Harrington
Production manager: Gordana Simakovic
Publishing manager: Penny Craig
Publisher: Cindy Richards

MIX
Paper from
responsible sources
FSC
www.fsc.org   FSC® C106563

CONTENTS

INTRODUCTION

I have always been a tea lover, ever since Auntie Edie taught me how important herbs are as I toddled behind her in her verdant kitchen garden. I was recently reminded of the deep healing of herbal brews, tinctures, and tonics after a bout of flu resulted in a lingering cough that would not go away, even after two trips to the doctor and several prescriptions. This in itself was a cause for worry. What was wrong with me? Nothing worked. In desperation, I studied the notes I'd made in my Book of Shadows on herbal remedies that had achieved good results and decided simply to double my intake of herbal tea. At the end of the first day, the cough was reduced and after a couple of days, no cough! Ever since, I have been evangelizing for drinking herbal brews. They have a power to heal when nothing else will.

We modern witches have a wealth of wisdom on which to draw, handed down to us from the wise women who were general practitioners for their village or tribe. An easy way to incorporate this into your life is to start keeping clean muslin or cheesecloth, big jars, and several colored glass bottles and canning jars with lids for storing your handiwork. We have centuries of recipes for potions and tonics that were used to help and heal the sick, birth babies, bind the wounded, and tend to fever and various other maladies. These hedge witches were healers who also helped with melancholy and related issues, which existed before the words stress, anxiety, and depression were ever applied to them. Perhaps Mother Nature is the ultimate wise women healer as she provides, and

has provided, an unlimited supply of natural medicines, which we can employ for mending mind, body, and spirit.

Tending and growing magical herbs and potent plants is a kind of botanical alchemy. I love how all-encompassing the creation of magic potions and teas can be: you start with a handful of seeds, tend your herb garden, and end up with a pantry filled with libations that are at once medicinal, delicious, celebratory, and, most importantly, crafted with loving care. The very act of gardening will be healing. You will learn what works in your spells and which herbs, teas, and plant-based potions and recipes will cause you and your loved ones to flourish. Healing magic is, of course, about far more than the spoken words of spells. The greater the clarity of intention and concentration you bring to bear, the more powerful your conjuring will be. Before you begin using any of the spells contained herein, think about the words and your intention, gathering energy from a place deep within.

Witches' brews are one of the most important aspects of house magic. Your garden grows plants, herbs, and fruits that are the source of delectable draughts and healing concoctions. These tonics comprise many kinds of teas, wines, ciders, and refreshments as well as medicinal tinctures, tisanes, infusions, and herbal vinegars. All made by your own hand, they will be a constant source of healing and delight to you and your circle.

CHAPTER 1

MAGICAL BREWING BASICS

A MUG OF MAGIC

The British and kitchen witches have one thing in common—they believe a good pot of tea can fix almost anything. And it is true—heartache, headaches, and all manner of ills seem to evaporate in the steam that rises from the spout of the kettle.

With a handful of herbs and a cauldron-full of witchy wisdom, big healing can result from a small cup of tea. Once you have the knack of that, you can also brew up simples, digestives, tisanes, tonics, tinctures, and the many other concoctions that can be created right at home. This is one of the most delightful aspects of kitchen witchery as these recipes are usually easy enough as long as you have the proper ingredients.

They make all the difference after a long day; they can be enjoyed alone and can also be shared to great effect. Bottled and hand-labeled, these potions also make significant gifts that will be long remembered for the thoughtfulness as well as the delight and comfort received. Prepare to brew up much joy.

SIMPLES

Teas brewed from a single herb are commonly called simples, a lovely phrase from olden times. Experience has taught me that simples often have the most potency; the purity of that single plant essence can come through undiluted. This book contains a plentitude of herbs you can use to brew tasty, helpful, and healing simples, but yarrow is one you should brew regularly.

Boil 2½ cups (590 ml) of distilled water. Place a half-ounce (15 g) of dried yarrow into your favorite crockery teapot and pour over the water. Steep for 10 minutes and strain with a non-metallic implement, such as an inexpensive bamboo strainer or cheesecloth (muslin). Sweeten with honey; clover honey intensifies the positivity of this potion and makes it a supremely lucky drink.

Yarrow brings courage, heart, and is a major medicine. All these aspects make yarrow one of the most strengthening of all simples.

STEEPED IN WISDOM

**Different kinds of tea can combine to make
a powerful concoction.**

A pot of your favorite grocer's black tea can become a magical potion
with the addition of a thin slice of ginger root and a pinch each of dried
chamomile and peppermint tea. This ambrosial brew can calm any
storm at home or at work. Before you drink a cup, pray:

This day I pray for calm and serenity for all,

Both within and without.

Give me the wisdom to see the beauty
of each waking moment.

Blessings abound to all I know.

So mote it be.

BLACK, GREEN, AND WHITE TEA

White tea, green tea, and black tea are all made from the leaves of *Camellia sinensis*.

White tea is made from the youngest leaves of the plant; it is a sweet brew and has less caffeine than green or black tea. It is also rich in antioxidants and is recommended for reducing "bad" cholesterol and improving artery health. White tea is a little costly, but a good choice for health and flavor. Use black tea for an upset tummy and headache. Green tea strengthens the immune system, and you can reuse tea bags to stanch cuts or calm insect bites.

MEDICINAL MAGIC

Herbal tea is truly a mainstay for wellbeing and has been for millennia. Brewing every morning can even be a deeply pleasant way to begin each day, as it is for me. I mix it up a few times each week in accordance with what I sense I will need for the day. Keep notes about what works for you and, after a while, you should have a good supply of different herbal teas you know bring you health and happiness.

I usually brew a large pot of tea and it can last through the day, going from hot in the morning to iced in the afternoon. Don't let your tea sit out at room temperature for too long, as it will go "flat," get tiny bubbles in it, and begin to sour. When stored in the refrigerator, an herbal tea will be good for three to four days.

A simple rule of thumb is to use 1–2 tablespoons of herb for each cup (240 ml) of water, or 4–6 tablespoons of herb per quart (liter) of water, unless it is a very strong herb.

For a medicinal tea to be effective, it must be administered in small amounts several times daily. For chronic problems, serve the tea three or four times daily. For acute ailments, such as colds, fevers, and headaches, take several small sips every 30 minutes until the symptoms subside.

POWERFUL HEALING HERBS

⋆ **Cold calmers:** Echinacea, elderberry, hibiscus, or nettle.

⋆ **Headache healers:** Chamomile, clove, peppermint, or willow bark.

⋆ **Fever fighters:** Bergamot, catnip, white willow bark, or yarrow.

⋆ **Stomach soothers:** Chamomile, fennel, ginger, holy basil, licorice (this is very strong so use only 1 teaspoon per cup of water), or mint.

⋆ **Sleep and serenity:** Lavender, lemon balm, lemongrass, passionflower, or valerian.

MAKING HERBAL TINCTURES

Tinctures have been used for millennia and are considered precious because they are so powerful. Tinctures are concentrated liquid extracts of herbs and are taken by the dropperful, most often diluted in warm water or juice. Because they are so potent, they should be administered carefully and sparingly.

For chronic problems, add ½ to 1 teaspoon of a tincture to a glass of warm water or juice three times daily. Any of the healing herbs in this book that you feel can help you can be made into tinctures with this easy recipe. The healthful benefits of the herb you select are magnified when adapted into a tincture—some marvelously witchy herbs for tinctures are suggested on page 18. There are several methods used to make tinctures, but the simplest method is the one I prefer.

GATHER TOGETHER

6 oz (170 g) fresh herbs, finely chopped

1 quart (1 liter) sealable jar, such as a Mason jar

3 cups (750 ml) solvent

CHOOSING A SOLVENT

Most tinctures are made with alcohol as the primary solvent. Although the amount of alcohol is very small, many people choose not to use alcohol-based tinctures for a variety of sound reasons, and excellent tinctures can be made with apple cider vinegar as the solvent. If you use alcohol, it should be 80- to 100-proof and the best options are vodka, gin, or brandy. Half of the proof number is the percentage of alcohol in the spirits: for example, 80-proof brandy is 40 percent alcohol; 100-proof vodka is 50 percent alcohol.

HERBS TO USE

Fresh herbs are usually used because they have much more potency, with a ratio of 1 part plant material to 4 parts liquid. If it is winter and only dry herbs are available, use 1 part dried plant material to 1 part liquid, though you may need some extra liquid to cover the herbs.

Add the herbs to the jar. Pour in the solvent, making sure to cover the herbs with an extra 3 in (7.5 cm) of liquid above them. Seal the jar tightly. Place the jar in a sunny and warm corner, such as on a windowsill. Keep there for at least a month—up to 6 weeks is ideal. Every day give the mixture a good shake.

Once you're ready, open the jar and strain through a clean, dry muslin or cheesecloth. Once well-strained, pour the remaining liquid into a small bottle or jar and store in a dark cupboard on a high shelf out of the reach of children. The strained herbs will make an excellent compost and this new brew will last nearly indefinitely.

PERFECT PICKS: HERBS FOR TINCTURES

All of us have particular affinities with certain plants, herbs, spices, and flowers. Experiment with each of your astrological tinctures until you find your favorite and the one that offers the most benefits to you.

 ★ **Aries** herbs are clove, cumin, fennel, juniper, and peppermint.

 ★ **Taurus** herbs are apple, rose, thyme, tonka bean, vanilla, and violet.

 ★ **Gemini** herbs are mint, clover, dill, lavender, lemongrass, and parsley.

 ★ **Cancer** herbs are lemon, lotus, and rose.

 ★ **Leo** herbs are cinnamon, heliotrope, nutmeg, orange, and rosemary.

 ★ **Virgo** herbs are almond, mint, and thyme.

 ★ **Libra** herbs are marjoram, mugwort, spearmint, and sweet pea.

 ★ **Scorpio** herbs are allspice, basil, cumin, galangal, and ginger.

 ★ **Sagittarius** herbs are anise, star anise, and honeysuckle.

 ★ **Capricorn** herbs are lemon thyme, lime, mimosa, and vervain.

 ★ **Aquarius** herbs are citron, lavender, and spearmint.

 ★ **Pisces** herbs are clover, blood orange, sarsaparilla, and sweet pea.

FLORAL ESSENCE ENERGIES

Many of our favorite flowers have distinctive healing energies that can be captured in water. A key difference between flower essences and essential oils is that flower essences minister to the emotional body while essential oils treat the physical body.

Vials of a multitude of flower essences are available at grocers, pharmacies, and new-age stores. Bach Flower Remedies are doubtless the most popular and have a recommended dosage of three to four drops taken via the bottle dropper under the tongue two to four times a day. I suggest using no more than two different floral waters at any given time for full effect.

Flower essences are typically ingested directly via the mouth or by way of adding a few drops to a glass of water. They can also be dropped onto linens, such as your pillowslip, or into your bath and can be applied directly to the pulse points (temples and wrists). Floral essences are also different from essential oils in that they do not carry the scent of the flower. It takes a few flowers to make an essence whereas essential oils rely on a significant amount of the plant. See page 108 for how to make your own flower essence.

THE HOMELY ART OF
HERBAL INFUSIONS

I heartily approve of the renewed popularity of these healthful
libations. Infusions are derived from the more fragile parts of
plants, which include the bud, flower, leaves, and scent-producing
parts. These delicate herbs require steeping rather than boiling or
simmering. They actually release their flavor more quickly than
tougher roots and barks.

GATHER TOGETHER

1 tablespoon herbs of your choice

Heat-resistant glass bowl

1 cup (240 ml) water

Teakettle

Add the herbs to the bowl. Boil the water, pour it over the herbs, and let
steep for 30 to 60 minutes. Strain into a mug, then enjoy either at room
temperature or reheated. The proportion of water to herb and the
required time to infuse varies greatly, depending on the herb. Start out
with the suggested proportions and then experiment. The more herb
you use and the longer you let it steep, the stronger the brew.

HERBS THAT HELP

★ **Chamomile** makes for sweet sleep and helps you attain a meditative state.

★ **Comfrey** is good for bones and skin renewal and will protect both you and your home.

★ **Echinacea** is known for curing colds, but it can also raise mood, immunity, and prosperity.

★ **Lavender** is a beloved therapeutic, but also brings mental strength and visionary thinking.

★ **Mint** sends anxiety and stress away and also calms your stomach.

★ **Mullein** is a wonderful aid for sleep and simple relaxing.

★ **Nettle** settles digestive ills, aches, and pains, while also enhancing psychic power.

★ **Oat straw** is a brain booster, helps reduce stress, and is a lesser-known love potion!

★ **Sage** is renowned for clearing energy, but also tames tension and abets longevity.

★ **Thyme** helps with letting go and overcoming grief and clears the lungs.

HERBAL INFUSION INVOCATION

**For any witch, the kitchen is the laboratory for alchemy.
The transference of the pure essence of an herb into oil or liqueur
is nothing less than magic. Adding the following step to the
process of infusing honors its alchemical aspect and adds
enchantment to the final product.**

After you have bottled up your infusions, and before you store them in
a dark pantry, place them on your altar. Check your almanac to see
what sign the sun and moon are in, and what the moon phase is. Have
a pretty label and a colored pen at the ready. Light a green candle, hold
one of the bottles in both hands, and pray aloud:

Under this moon and sun,

Green magic binds into one.

By my hand, I filled this bottle with grace,

To bring enjoyment to all who come to this place.

Blessings for all; and so be it.

Take the pen and write on
the label the kind of herbal oil
or liquer you have made.
For example:

APPLE BRANDY SPIRITS
Made on June 15,
under the Gemini Sun
and Taurus New Moon

PANTRY POWER

Many enjoy daily cups of their favorite herbal infusion, which is a large portion of herb brewed for at least four hours and as long as ten.

I recommend one cup of the dried herb placed in a quart-canning jar and filled with freshly boiled water. After the steeping, strain using a non-metallic method, such as cheesecloth or bamboo. Herbal infusions can be made with the leaves and fruits that provide the magical and healing aspects of this comforting concoction. Many of the favorite kitchen witch herbs contain minerals, antioxidants, and phytochemicals. Roots, leaves, flowers, needles, and seeds can all be used—depending on which fruit or herb is chosen to be the base. There are some cases when all parts of the plant can be used in some manner, and for others only one or two parts are safe—it is important, when creating a blend from scratch, to research the ingredients to understand what parts can be used.

BLESSINGS ON A BUDGET

Instead of composting all the herbs, twigs, and stems from your brews, you can store them in a burlap or hessian sack and allow them to dry. Keep stuffing it until you have a big bag. On a special evening, burn it in your fireplace or an outdoor bonfire and it will be like a gigantic incense burner with lovely scents wafting from the flames.

HERBS AND ASSOCIATIONS

★ **Anise** seeds and leaves soothe cramps and aches.

★ **Caraway** seeds aid in romantic issues and help with colic.

★ **Catnip** leaves increase attractiveness.

★ **Chamomile** flowers help with sleep and are good for abundance.

★ **Dandelion** leaves make wishes come true.

★ **Echinacea** makes the body strong.

★ **Ginseng** root increases men's vigor.

★ **Nettle** leaves are good for lung function and hex breaking.

★ **Peppermint** leaves rid tummy discomfort and are cleansing.

★ **Pine** needles increase skin health as well as financial health.

★ **Rose hip** fruit is packed with vitamin C and can halt colds and flu.

★ **Sage** leaves purify energy and are a natural antibiotic.

★ **Skullcap** leaves cure insomnia, headaches, anxiety, and nervous tension.

★ **St John's wort** leaves act as an anti-depressant and provide protection.

★ **Thyme** leaves are antiseptic and a protectant.

★ **Yarrow** flowers reduce fever and bring courage and good luck.

DANDY SASSAFRAS GINGER DETOX

When I was little, living on the family farm, I accompanied my part-Cherokee dad to the woods, looking for sassafras roots to make tea. I loved the taste; it was delightful and also gave me more energy.

After apprenticing with my dad for a few years, he allowed me to go out alone, gathering the source of my dearly beloved beverage. Years later, I discovered that sassafras was highly prized by Native Americans who used it for medicine and who were extremely knowledgeable about combining herbs to amplify their power.

This morning medicine is inspired by a shamanic native-healing recipe using sassafras roots, dandelion greens, and slices of wild ginger. For a wonderfully medicinal decoction, take a half-cup of each and boil them in distilled water. After steeping for 12 minutes, stir in honey and enjoy. It is pleasantly surprising how good the detox tastes and even more how the herbs combine to eliminate toxins from the body, chiefly the kidney and liver.

During the holidays or pagan-feast times, we all imbibe and enjoy rich foods, good wine, and sugary desserts. This purifying herbal blend will cleanse the organs that cleanse your body, thus aiding wellness. This detox should be used seasonally and is not intended for daily use, due to its great power.

DECOCTIONS 101

Roots, bark, and herbs with tough stems and seeds don't really lend themselves to the method of infusing. Decocting is boiling and then evaporating by simmering slowly to produce the most concentrated liquid, which is excellent in medicines. Use a coffee grinder for roots and small pieces of bark and stems to make quick work of these. I recommend the decoction method for the roots of willow, sarsaparilla, wild cherry, yohimbe, yucca, licorice, parsley, dandelion, angelica, and cohosh.

NURTURE THROUGH NATURE

GARDENER'S TEA

As you may know, tilling the backyard and harvesting your herbs and veggies is a huge amount of work. It is one of life's greatest joys, without doubt, but nevertheless, many a sore back and aching knees have come as result of a thriving garden. All the more reason for tea that revives, refreshes, and offers relief to aching joints.

GATHER TOGETHER

2 parts dried echinacea

2 parts dried chamomile

1 part dried mint

1 part anise seed

1 part dried thyme

Gather the ingredients from your store of dried herbs and add boiling water. Allow to steep, then strain into a cup. A nice hot cup of this remedy will have you jumping back into the garden to plant more of all the herbs that comprise this delightful tea. Ahh, sit back and enjoy. You deserve it!

BALM FOR ALL SORROWS

Lemon balm also goes by the equally lovely Latinate Melissa. From Greco-Roman times, this relative of the mint family has been held as a significant medicine.

You can grow lemon balm with ease from seed packets in almost any kind of soil, but it likes shade in the afternoon to prevent wilting. This is one of the happy plants that will "volunteer" and spread in your garden and can be used in love magic—to bring love to you and also heal after a break-up or divorce. It can also be employed as an aphrodisiac.

Infusions and teas made from lemon balm make good on the offer the name implies—it can soothe the heart and any lingering upset, blue moods, and aches and pains from trauma, both physical and emotional. We should all grow as much as possible and let some of it go to seed for those new plants that will pop up in unexpected places in your herb garden. A kitchen witch never complains about a plentitude of balm; anyone who makes much use of lemon balm in brews and cookery will enjoy an abundance of love.

THYME TINCTURE

Every kitchen witch's garden should be strewn with thyme, growing among the flagstones in the path, and also in the rows of herbs, filling the air with its magnificent scent and elegant beauty.

You will need to keep a plentitude growing and several bunches drying in a dark corner of your pantry at all times as this plant makes a mighty fine tincture with many medicinal uses. I also suggest you start keeping clean muslin or cheesecloth, big jars, and several colored glass bottles and canning jars with lids for storing your handiwork.

GATHER TOGETHER

1¼ cups (65 g) dried thyme leaves

2 cups (480 ml) apple cider vinegar

For this tincture, take one of the larger jars. Put the dried thyme in the jar and carefully pour the vinegar inside. Stir well and seal. Place on a dark shelf and shake it every day. At the end of one month, strain through cheesecloth (muslin). Compost the thyme residue in your garden and store the tincture in a pretty glass jar.

Having this herbal helper around will come in handy for mouthwashes, hair rinses, and ritual baths—you can even use it to rub on achy joints and sore muscles. For a cup of thyme tea, add one teaspoon of the tincture into a cup of hot water, add a teaspoon of honey, stir, and enjoy.

MIRACLE SALVE

Thyme in the garden attracts bees and honey made by these "thyme-ly bees" is highly sought after. If you can come by this rarity, get as much as you can as it is redolent of Mother Nature's love and enchantment. The ancient Greeks prized this very highly, not only as a delicacy at the table, but also as a miracle salve to heal everything: the stomach, aches, and pains, and even wounds. Hippocrates swore by it!

LUXURIATING IN LAVENDER

Lavender is hard not to grow, and once your seedlings and young plants have been established, they will bush out and produce loads of scented stalks, flowers, and seeds. This bounty will become your source for teas, tinctures, bath salts, and infusions.

For tea, the rule of thumb is one teaspoon dried lavender flowers to one cup (240 ml) boiling water to aid tummy trouble, headache, aches, insomnia, and even to help calm the mind. You can easily amp up the therapeutic power of your brew by adding any of these excellent herbs—dried yarrow, St John's wort, or chamomile.

This is a simple and streamlined way to infuse lavender: pour a heaping tablespoon into a bowl of hot water and then drape a towel over your head and breathe in the aromatic fumes to deal with respiratory issues, coughs, colds, headaches, stuffy sinuses, and nervous tension. You will come away feeling renewed and your kitchen will smell like the heavens above.

You can use the water in your morning bath or add to your sink garbage disposal; grinding up the flowers refreshes that hard-duty kitchen appliance.

LAVENDER TINCTURE

This cure-all should be kept on hand at all times for soothing the skin, the stomach, and anything in need of comfort. I have even seen it used to stanch bleeding in small cuts.

GATHER TOGETHER

Clear quart (liter) jar with lid

Dried lavender

1 cup (240 ml) clear alcohol, such as vodka

2 cups (480 ml) distilled water

Cheesecloth (muslin)

Dark glass jar or bottle for storage

Fill your clear jar to the halfway point with the dried lavender. Pour in the alcohol also to the halfway point. Add in the water, seal securely with a lid, and shake for a few minutes until it seems well mixed. Store in a dark cupboard for one month, shaking once a day.

After 30 days, strain through the cheesecloth into the dark glass storage jar and screw the lid on tightly. The lavender leavings will make lovely compost and the liquid tincture will soon prove itself indispensable in your household.

MINT: REFRESH YOUR MENTAL POWERS

Another useful herb is mint, which is so easily grown that a little bunch in the backyard can go on to become a scented, attractive groundcover.

It is also called the flower of eternal refreshment. Woven into a laurel, it bestows brilliance, artistic inspiration, and prophetic ability. As a tea, it accomplishes miracles of calming the stomach and the mind at the same time.

TEA LEAF TONER MIST

Having this bracingly minty toner on hand will be an enchanting refresher whenever you need it.

GATHER TOGETHER

2 teaspoons peppermint leaves

2 teaspoons white sage tea

French press (cafetière)

½ cup (120 ml) boiled distilled water

3 drops lavender essential oil

4 fl oz (110 ml) aloe vera gel

6 fl oz (170 ml) spray bottle

Place the peppermint and tea leaves into the French press and then pour the freshly boiled water over the herbs. Let steep for 10 minutes, then add the lavender essential oil drops. Pour the aloe vera gel into the spray bottle, followed by the warm herbal tea, and seal the bottle. Shake well and refrigerate.

Anytime you need a mood shift or to feel restored, spritz the mist on your face, and even your arms and legs. You will feel refreshed instantly.

SPICY ROSE HIPS TONIC

We all love rose blossoms but what remains after the petals are long gone is just as good and bursting with vitamin C. Adding other healthful herbs to them makes this drink a delightful energy and wellness boost.

GATHER TOGETHER

4 parts dried rose hips

2 parts dried rose geranium leaves

2 parts dried dandelion leaves

1 chopped cinnamon stick

Mixing bowl

Sealable jar, such as a Mason jar

Simply mix all the herbs gently in the bowl, then transfer to the jar. This excellent tea can be placed into your tea ball or small muslin bag for an invigorating brew that will put the bloom of the rose on your cheek!

Enjoy the abundant gifts of Mother Nature's apothecary.

GETTING HYGGE WITH YOUR HONEY

We might call it kitchen witchery and our Scandinavian friends could say it is how we "get hygge," which means to get as cozy as humanly possible. This newly trendy lifestyle tradition from the frozen north is not just for lazing about, though we greatly appreciate that aspect; it is also a very healthy way of living that includes lots of herbal food and drink, shared with your sweetheart, which is an immunity booster on its own. Tea is always a mainstay. For an ambrosial brew you can enjoy together, add a sliver of ginger root and a pinch each of echinacea and mint to a cup of hot black tea. Add a teaspoon of honey—then relax and enjoy together!

FULL MOON TEA

It amuses me to see how trendy cold-brewed tea has become as hedgewitches and wise women have been making this delightful concoction for centuries. It is made in the same way as Sun Tea, which is gently heated by the warmth of the sun, but is brewed at night in the light of the moon.

GATHER TOGETHER

1 quart (1 liter) canning jar with lid

Cold, pure distilled water

4 herbal teabags or 3 heaping tablespoons of dried herbs of your choice

Large tea ball or small muslin bag (if using dried herbs)

Fill the jar with the distilled water and add the herbal teabags (or the tea ball/muslin bag filled with the dried herbs). Seal the lid on the canning jar and leave it outside or on your windowsill so it can be exposed to the light of the moon. When you awaken in the morning, you will have cold-brewed tea.

Do make notes in your Book of Shadows for which brews taste best to you. I can tell you that when the full moon is in the signs of Taurus, Cancer, Virgo, Libra, or Pisces, the tea is most delicious to me, with my current favorites being ginger peach and cinnamon hibiscus.

HERBS FOR FULL MOON TEAS

Here are a few suggestions for herbs and plants to use for your Full Moon Tea, as well as Sun Tea and traditional tea.

★ **Beautiful blue borage:** This sweetly blue flower has long been used to decorate cakes and other sweets, but also has a light and pleasant flavor that makes for a lovely, fruity tea. You might want to grow borage in your garden because it attracts pollinators such as bees. Borage tea is very calming and is a marvelous anti-inflammatory.

★ **Delicious dandelion:** The gardener's bane should actually be greeted gladly, as these humble yellow weeds are superfoods! They make a hearty and healthy tea, and are excellent as salad greens, so you can take advantage of all the nutrients. If that was not enough, dandelions can also be used to make excellent wine!

★ **Helpful hyssop:** Both the beautiful purple flowers of hyssop and its leaves have a tangy licorice flavor. This true medicinal can be used from stem to leaf to flower for brewing soothing teas to relieve pain, quiet respiratory complaints, and support your digestion.

★ **Noble nasturtiums:** These are one of my favorites, because anyone can grow them anywhere. They reseed themselves, so you only need to plant them once and you will have a salad green, a spicy tea, and gorgeous flowers that cheer you up every time you see them.

The leaves of the sun-colored flower can be dried and brewed in a tea that is packed with vitamin C and is capable of both healing and preventing colds and flu.

★ **Loveliest lavender:** So versatile, this herb is an absolute necessity in healing magic. While it is nearly universally used as an oil, lotion, and aromatic, it is often forgotten that it makes for a terrific tea. Add bergamot and you will get both an energy boost and a sense of calm. In this case, just breathing in the scent of lavender tea will bring serenity and wellbeing.

★ **Radiant rose:** I have an old-fashioned rose with gorgeous orange blossoms that has a tangy scent that is spectacular. Flavors vary depending on the variety and growing conditions, so petals can be both spicy and sweet, but in general darker petals have more flavor. Brewed into a tea and sweetened with honey, rose will attract love into your life and a sense of self-love as well. The scent and energy of rose is very gentle and will raise your vibration and uplift your personal energy.

★ **Vivid violet:** This tea might be the most unusual of all, as it has an enchanted color and can be used to brew a lovely blue-green tea that helps with pain relief, insomnia, and coughs. Johnny jump-ups and their cousin pansy can be used as well. Utterly charming and good for you, too!

WELLNESS WEEDS

Make the most of Mother Nature's medicine cabinet! These classic healing herbs can all be found in your local health store or online.

★ **Ashwagandha *(Withania somnifera)*:** Gently simmer 1 tablespoon of dried and minced ashwagandha root in 1 cup (240 ml) water for 8–10 minutes. Strain and sip once or twice a day as a rejuvenating tonic, anti-inflammatory, anxiety reducer, and immunity reducer.

★ **Black cohosh *(Actaea racemosa)*:** Make a tincture and take 1–2 milliliters three times a day to relieve menstrual cramps and arthritic pain. Black cohosh can also help peri- and menopausal symptoms.

★ **Calendula *(Calendula officinalis)*:** Boil 1 cup (240 ml) water and pour over two teaspoons of calendula petals. Steep this for 8–10 minutes and strain. Once it has cooled enough, you can drink it as tea, or use it as a mouthwash or gargle with it to reduce any swelling of the mouth or throat.

★ **Elderberry _(Sambucus nigra_ ssp. _canadensis)_:** This time-tested medicinal has long been used for guarding against colds and flu. Elderberry flowers have been valued as a tonic for fever for centuries; such fruit extracts have been proven to be noteworthy antivirals, especially against immunity issues. Two teaspoons of dried flowers in 1 cup (240 ml) boiling water three times a day does the trick—sweeten with local honey to taste.

★ **Ginger root _(Zingiber officinale)_:** From tummy troubles to colds and flus, ginger is beloved for its curative powers. Any greengrocer or herbal apothecary will have plenty of ginger root in stock, which you should always have around. When anyone in your family feels nauseous or a

LOCAL HONEY HEALS!

Why local? Allergies can exacerbate any cold or respiratory issue. Many who suffer seasonal allergies have found local, raw honey to be wonderful as it desensitizes them to the flora triggering their allergic reaction. Twice as sweet!

cold or fever coming, slice and mince a tablespoon of the root in 1 cup (240 ml) hot water for tea. Steep to taste and drink twice a day for a surprisingly swift end to your suffering.

★ **Ginseng** *(Panax quinquefolius; Panax ginseng)*: Many people rely upon ginseng to relieve and avert mental and physical fatigue. This herb has been shown to reduce the occurrence and acuteness of colds. Some even claim it can help with issues of male virility. Simmer 1 teaspoon, either dried or fresh, in 1 cup (240 ml) freshly boiled water for 8–10 minutes three times a day.

★ **Hibiscus** *(Hibiscus sabdariffa)*: Beloved for the heavenly sweet perfume of the flowers, hibiscus is also a powerful diuretic and can lower blood pressure. As if that is not enough, it can also help sore throats and colds. Similar to other herbal applications, steep a tablespoon of the dried flowers in 1 cup (240 ml) freshly boiled water for 10 minutes and drink twice a day.

★ **Garlic** *(Allium sativum)*: We have all heard that the Chinese praise garlic for the health benefits. It is a powerful antimicrobial, often employed to combat colds, ease sinus congestion, and stave off digestion problems that accompany traveling. It has even been shown that regular use can help gently lower blood pressure. 1–2 fresh cloves are the dose.

★ **Kava kava** *(Piper methysticum)*: This root is said to be highly effective as a muscle relaxer and for reducing anxiety. Kava can be handled the same as ginger, with 1 tablespoon of minced root or dried root taken as tea. I recommend seeing how it affects you before you raise the dose to the recommended amounts of 2 or 3 cups of tea per day.

★ **Licorice** *(Glycyrrhiza glabra)*: This revered candy classic is also a wonderful anti-inflammatory which relieves the discomfort of colds in the sinuses. It can ease sore throats and coughs, and is also a tummy soother that is good for gut health. Use licorice root as you would ginger, with 1 minced teaspoon of fresh or dried root steeped in 1 cup (240 ml) freshly boiled water twice a day.

★ **Marshmallow** *(Althaea officinalis)*: While it may seem like this is another "candy as medicine," marshmallow is a time-tested plant long employed in field medicine. It is greatly valued as it contains a high amount of mucilage, which contains many beneficial antioxidants. Minced fresh or dried root or the leaves are equally healing. Use ¼ cup (10 g) in 1 cup (240 ml) water, steeped for 4 hours. Strain out the stems and drink hot or cool, sweetened or unsweetened— however you like this gentle herb.

Look to the natural world to heal
your mind, body, and soul.

★ **Milk thistle** *(Silybum marianum):* Healers love milk thistle for its ability to protect the liver from toxins, harsh medicines, alcohol, and unseen environmental pollutants. It can be obtained as an extract at any health food store or upscale grocery or pharmacy. There is some evidence it can also help improve kidney conditions.

★ **Mullein** *(Verbascum thapsus):* Here is an herbalist's favorite for healing any respiratory ailment involving congestion, coughs, and sore throats, that can also calm the breathing. Mullein flowers infused in oil are also used to aid earaches. Steep one heaping tablespoon of the leaves in 1 cup (240 ml) boiling water for no more than 10 minutes. After one cup of tea, you'll feel better soon.

★ **Nettle** *(Urtica dioica):* Nettle has been used as a healer for untold centuries and it relieves allergies, boosts the immune system, and can even help with a distended prostate. It is also a superfood and beloved for its nutrients. If you are working with fresh nettles, wear gloves to avoid the stings. Cooking or drying removes any irritant. Any herb or health food store will have dried nettle or nettles in a capsule form. Make nettle tea by steeping 2 teaspoons of leaves in 1 cup (240 ml) freshly boiled water for 10 minutes, or take the capsules in recommended doses of 300–500 mg twice a day.

COMPOST TEA

Compost tea is a marvelous way to feed your plants and give them extra nutrients in a wholly natural way that is free of chemicals.

You want to feed your friends and family clean, pesticide-free produce, so start out organic and you will soon have a garden that produces healthy food.

GATHER TOGETHER

2 cups (400 g) fresh, homemade compost from your compost bin, pile, or garden center

1 gallon (3.75 liters) clean, filtered water

Put the compost and water in a large bucket and place out of direct heat or cold—I use my shed, but a garage will also do nicely. Let your compost tea "brew" for a week and give it a stir every other day. When the time is up, strain out the dirt and pour the liquid into your watering can—the perfect garden teapot—to serve up some serious nutrients to your plants.

BLESSING FOR HERBAL MEDICINE

At the guidance of a master herbalist with whom I apprenticed,
I learned to consecrate the remedies I was making, which adds to
their efficacy. Herbal healing is a sacred art and invoking the
power of nature will strengthen your homemade magic.

Great-hearted goddess of
earth so green

We give thanks for your
generosity, O Queen.

You give us everything we
need to live.

To you, much love and
gratitude we give.

Blessed be.

CHAPTER 3

SOOTHING SIPS

CONJURING BY THE CUP

Tea is not only a delectable drink, but also of equal importance are the great healing powers contained in each cup. Growing and drying herbs for your own kitchen-witchery brews is truly one of life's simple pleasures. Tea conjures a very powerful alchemy because, when you drink it, you take the magic inside of you.

For an ambrosial brew with the power to calm any storm, add a sliver of ginger root and a teaspoon each of chamomile and peppermint to two cups of boiling water. Let steep and, as the mixture brews and cools, pray using the following words:

This day I pray for strength and health,

And the wisdom to see the beauty in each waking moment.

Blessings abound; good health is true wealth.

GREEN WITCHERY
HEALTHY BREWS

Herbal tea nourishes the soul, heals the body, and calms the mind. Try any of the following:

★ **Blackberry** leaf tea reduces mood swings and evens glucose levels, thus aiding weight management. This miraculous herbal even helps circulation and aids such issues as inflammation and varicose veins. It is helpful to cancer patients and is believed to be a preventative.

★ **Catnip** is one of the witchiest of teas and is not only grown as fun for your feline familiar. At the first inkling of a sore throat or impending cold, drink a warm cup of catnip tea and head off to bed. You will awaken feeling much better. Catnip soothes the nervous system and can safely help get a restless child go off to sleep as it's a gentle but potent sleep-inducer.

★ **Fennel** is excellent for awakening and uplifting and is great for digestion and cleansing. Fennel is also a natural breath freshener.

★ **Cardamom** is a favorite of expectant mothers everywhere as it calms nausea and morning sickness; this east-India fragrant is excellent for digestion and clears and cleans your mouth and throat. Anyone who likes cinnamon will love cardamom.

★ **Nettle** raises your energy level, boosts the immune system, and is packed with iron and vitamins.

★ **Echinacea** lends an increased and consistent sense of wellbeing and prevents colds and flu. It is a very powerful immune booster.

★ **Ginger** root calms and cheers while aiding digestion and nausea and can also fend off coughs and sore throats.

★ **Dandelion** root grounds and centers, providing many minerals and nutrients. This wonderful weed is also a cleanser and a wholly natural detoxifier.

SOUL-SOOTHING TEA SPELL

The pace and pressures of daily life, not to mention the incoming news, can take a toll.

We can become ungrounded and lose our center due to the stressors from the outer world, which calls for reconnecting to nature through herbal remedies. This gentlest of teas belies the great strength of this combination to restore both body and soul.

GATHER TOGETHER

Teakettle filled with freshly drawn water

2 tablespoons dried chamomile

1 tablespoon dried catnip

1 tablespoon dried lemon balm

Large tea ball or small muslin bag

Teapot

1 sprig fresh mint

Mug

While the kettle is on the boil, add the dried herbs
to the bag or tea ball and speak this blessing:

Herbs of the goddess,
replenish me this day.

Water of the river,
restore me this way.

I reclaim my tranquility now, I say.

Blessed be to all. Blessings to me.

Pour the boiled water into the teapot
and let steep for 5 minutes to get the full power
of these mildest herbs. Take the fresh mint sprig and crush it
in the bottom of the mug to release the pure essence of the plant. Pour
a cup of the tea and speak the blessing once more. Now sip slowly,
making sure to take in the stillness and serenity the brew offers. I have
gotten into the habit of drinking more than one mugful in a sitting, and I
recommend the same for you. Anytime you need to regain your center
and calm, this tea is a sure path to peace of mind.

ELDERBERRY WISDOM BLEND

One cup of this per day will help you sleep, alleviate anxiety, help aches and pains, and sharpen your mind. Elderberry as a medicinal was especially prized by Druids, who studied flora deeply and regarded elderberry as a holy tree.

GATHER TOGETHER

2 teaspoons dried elderberries

2 teaspoons dried hawthorn berries

1 teaspoon fresh blackberries

1 teaspoon dried raspberry leaf

Small bowl

Large tea ball or small muslin bag

Teakettle filled with freshly drawn water

Ceramic teapot

Honey, to taste

Place all the berries and herbs into the bowl and mix well. Place in a large tea ball or a clean and dry muslin bag in the ceramic teapot. Bring your teakettle to a boil, pour the water over the herbs, and let steep for five minutes. Sweeten to taste with honey—clover honey is especially good. Speak this chant before you drink:

Spirits of nature, bless these herbs,

So we may never be unwell.

Spirits of the Harvest, bless this brew,

So we may leave all worry and woe. And so it is.

GINGER LEMON WINE

For most of us, ginger is our go-to for stomach-settling tea, but wine made from this wholesome root offers the very same benefit. It will also warm you at night and abet easy and peaceful sleep.

GATHER TOGETHER

½ cup (50 g) fresh ginger root, chopped

Large lidded pan

Wooden spoon

2 gallons (7.5 liters) fresh water

5 cups (1 kg) granulated sugar

Juice of 3 lemons

½ cup (125 ml) honey

Large bowl

Strainer

Large corked bottle

Label and pen

Bruise the ginger by mashing it with the wooden spoon in the pan. Add half the water and bring to a slow boil. Stir well and place the lid on the pan. Turn the heat down to simmer for 30 minutes, then remove from the heat and let it cool for ten minutes.

Pour the sugar, lemon juice, and honey into a bowl and stir well with the wooden spoon. Now pour the ginger mixture into the bowl. Boil the remaining water, add to the bowl, and stir until the sugar is completely dissolved and all is thoroughly mixed. Now strain the liquid back into the pan and then again back into the bowl.

Pour the strained ginger lemon liquid into the bottle and label it. For example, if the moon is new and in the sign of Gemini, add that to your label so it reads: Gemini New Moon Ginger Lemon Wine. Let it set for 24 hours and, after that, it is good to go. Drink it chilled or warm for an inner glow.

GINGER
LEMON WINE

GEMINI NEW MOON

RESTORATIVE FULL MOON INFUSION

The full moon is a truly auspicious time and one to savor and make the most of. Try this restorative Lunar Elixir anytime your energy level is low to bolster mind, body, and spirit. The full moon phases last two days, so it's best to make this elixir on the first night at midnight.

GATHER TOGETHER

1 teaspoon sliced fresh ginger root

1 teaspoon jasmine tea leaves

1 teaspoon peppermint tea leaves

2 cups (480 ml) freshly drawn water

Teapot

Mug

Just before midnight, brew and strain an infusion of these healthful and energizing herbs. Once it is cool, pour it into your favorite mug and relish the aromatic steam for a moment. Wait for the stroke of midnight. Now, step outside and drink the elixir during this enchanted hour in the glow of moonlight. You will immediately feel clearer, more centered, and more focused.

AN AMBROSIAL BREW

For an ambrosial brew with the power to calm any storm, add a sliver of ginger root and a pinch each of echinacea and mint to a cup of hot black tea. Before you drink, pray:

This day I pray for calm, for health, for clarity

For me and all others.

I pray for the wisdom to see the beauty
of each waking moment.

Blessing be. Blessings for all.

Every day, you can renew your
own health and wellness in many
small ways; a cup of green tea
with a morning prayer can be a
simple rite that gives you calm
and greater wellness.

CHAPTER 4

DELIGHTFUL DRINKS

JASMINE JOY RITUAL

Jasmine tea is a delightful concoction and can create an aura of bliss and conviviality.

It is available at any grocer or purveyor of organic goods, but homegrown is even better. Brew a cup of jasmine tea and let it cool. Add two parts lemonade to one part jasmine tea and drink the mixture with a good friend. Jasmine is a vine and represents the intertwining of people. You will be more bonded to anyone with whom you share this sweet ritual.

This is also a tonic that you can indulge in when alone. I recommend brewing up a batch every Monday, or "Moon Day," to ensure that each week is filled with joyfulness. As the jasmine tea steeps, pray:

On this Moon Day in this new week,

I call upon the spirits to guide
joy to my door.

By this moon on this day, I call upon
Selene, goddess fair

To show me the best way to live.

For this, I am grateful.

Blessed be the brew; blessed be me.

MERRY MEET
MEDIEVAL BREW

This special mixture is created by mixing a gallon (3.8 liters) of unfiltered sweet apple cider into a cauldron. You can buy the cider but it is even better if you make it from apples you have gathered or harvested (see page 104).

Take a bottle of your favorite low-cost red wine and heat gently in the pot on a low flame; add sugar, cinnamon, and cloves to your taste, but at least a tablespoon of each. Pour the cider into the warmed wine and add 13 whole cloves and 6 cinnamon sticks, then stir widdershins (counterclockwise) every six minutes. Notice how your entire home fills with the spicy sweetness of merriment. After 30 minutes, your brew should be ready to serve.

HOOF AND HORN RITE

If indoor-bound on Beltane Eve, pick a place with a fireplace, so celebrants can wear comfy clothing and dance barefoot.

Ask them to bring spring flowers and musical instruments. Serve a spread of finger foods, honeyed mead, beer, spiced cider, wine, and fruity teas. As you light incense, set out green, red, and white candles, one for each participant. When it is time to call the circle, raise your arm and point to each direction, saying "To the east, to the north," etc., then sing:

Hoof and horn, hoof and horn,

Tonight our spirits are reborn. [repeat thrice]

Welcome, joy, to this home.

Fill these friends with love and laughter,

So mote it be.

Have each guest light a candle and speak to the subject of love with a toast of Beltane Brew (see page 136). Drumming and dancing is the next part of the circle. This is truly an invocation of lust for life, now rejoice!

ELEMENT OF AIR TONIC

This spell provides brilliant insight, peace, and clarity. It works best when the new moon is in an Air sign: Aquarius, Gemini, or Libra.

GATHER TOGETHER

1 tablespoon fenugreek seeds

4 tablespoons fresh peppermint leaves

Pinch of dried lavender

Yellow teapot

Honey

Steep the herbs in boiling water in your teapot. After 5 minutes, sweeten with honey, and either drink the mild tea or pour it on the ground outside while facing east, the source of the rising sun. Pray:

Winged Mercury, God of air,

I entreat you to bring me sight and true awareness.

Like the wind, speed my way.

A CUP BRIMMING
WITH HEALTH

This tonic provides bioflavonoids and vitamin C in an organic, natural way so all the nutrients are easily available for absorption. Drink this blend regularly and you will feel fantastic.

The amounts of ingredients are given in parts, as you may want to make a big batch of tea for the whole family.

GATHER TOGETHER

2 parts lemongrass

3 parts hibiscus

4 parts rose hips

1 part chopped cinnamon sticks

Teapot

Honey

Blend the herbs using your mortar and pestle. Place in a teapot with 4 cups (960 ml) of hot water. Steep for 5 minutes in your teapot, then strain and serve sweetened with honey to taste. Serve regularly as a preventative during cold and flu season.

CHICORY ROOT CHEER

I love triple lattes, but they keep me awake into the night and then, in order to function well in the morning, I have to get back on the coffee grind to keep going.

Chicory has a similarly wonderful flavor to coffee, but it is caffeine-free and easier on the system. It is a commonly found bright blue wildflower, a member of the daisy family, but it is the parsnip-like roots that are what we use for roasting and grinding. You can find chicory roots at any natural grocery and you might become such a fan that you will take a long break from coffee.

GATHER TOGETHER

Bunch of fresh organic chicory

Sharp knife

Roasting pan

Clean, dry cloth

Coffee grinder

Coffee maker

Mug

Milk and/or sugar, to taste

Preheat the oven to 325°F/170°C/Gas 3. Rinse the chicory roots well in cool water. Cut them into small cubes and let dry on the cloth. Once the roots are dry, place them on the roasting pan and heat for a half hour. Toward the end of the cooking time, you should smell a delightful coffee-like scent. Take out the roasted roots and let them cool. Grind the root pieces like you would coffee beans and brew. I suggest you try your first cup of chicory coffee plain, so you taste the true earthy flavor of the root. In addition to giving your body a break from the stress of caffeine, chicory is very good for detoxing and is less well known for its magical properties of strength, good luck, frugality, and the removal of obstacles and curses.

BRAIN AND BODY BOOSTER

We all need a pick-me-up once in a while, especially by the end of the week when our physical and emotional tank might be empty. This wild and spicy brew will soon have you moving and grooving again!

GATHER TOGETHER

Teakettle

1 quart (1 liter) freshly drawn water

2 teaspoons fresh nettle

½ teaspoon ginkgo

1 teaspoon fresh or dried licorice

1 teaspoon chopped cinnamon stick

1 teaspoon finely diced fresh ginger root

Mortar and pestle

1 quart (1 liter) sealable jar, such as a Mason jar

While you are boiling the water in the kettle, place the herbs into your mortar and grind them together until well-mixed. Transfer the ground herbs to the jar and pour in the boiling water. Steep for a half hour, then strain. The yield should be enough for three big glasses. I suggest you drink one glass while still warm and store and refrigerate the rest in the jar.

The recommended dose per day is three glasses a day in the morning, at lunchtime, and after dinner, twice a week. If you are feeling really run down, drink it every other day and you'll pep up quite soon!

HOT TODDY HEALING

When someone needs cheering up after a long day or is going through hard times, I mix up a quick hot toddy, adding in one of my tonics or tinctures—I keep a constant supply of echinacea and goldenseal tonic for the purpose, using the same recipe as for lavender and chamomile.

A hot toddy is traditionally made with hot water, lemon, sugar or honey, and liquor. The herbal tonic adds a higher level of medicinal power, and I also take it at the first sign of a cold or cough.

GATHER TOGETHER

1 tablespoon pure honey

2 teaspoons fresh lemon juice

½ cup (120 ml) hot water or brewed tea

1 fl oz (30 ml) brandy or bourbon

Lemon or fresh ginger root slice

10 drops of lavender and chamomile tonic (see page 102)

Mug

Warm your mug by
pouring boiling water into it and
letting it sit for 2 minutes.
Pour away the hot water and put in
the honey and lemon juice. Add hot water
or tea and stir until the honey has dissolved.
Add the brandy or bourbon, stir, and drop in a lemon
slice. A slice of ginger can be substituted for the
lemon for extra zing. To finish, add the lavender and
chamomile tonic and stir. Nothing is more reassuring
than a warm drink served with love.

CINNAMON LIQUEUR

This popular pagan beverage gives peppy energy and can also be a love potion. These few ingredients can lead to a lifetime of devotion.

GATHER TOGETHER

1 cup (240 ml) vodka

2 cloves

1 teaspoon ground coriander seed

1 cinnamon stick

1 cup (240 ml) simple sugar syrup

Pour the vodka into a bowl and add the herbs. Cover with a clean, dry towel and place in a cupboard for two weeks. Strain and filter until the result is a clear liquid into which you add the simple syrup and place back on the shelf for a week.

Store this in a pink- or red-capped bottle; you now have liquid love. You can add this to hot chocolate, water, tea, or milk for a delightful drink to share with a partner.

PASSION POTION SPELL

Lower the lamps, light red candles, and enjoy a warm cup of cocoa with a shot of the cinnamon liqueur. Speak this spell aloud as you are preparing the libation—you will radiate passion and draw your lover to you with this enchantment:

Today, I awaken the goddess in me.

By surrendering to my love for thee.

Tonight, I will heat the night with my fire.

As we drink this cup, we awaken desire.

I am alive! I am love. So mote it be.

LOVER'S TEA

**Here is a quick recipe to create exactly the right mood
for a dreamy evening.**

GATHER TOGETHER

1 oz (30 g) dried hibiscus flowers

1 oz (30 g) dried and pulverized rose hips

½ oz (15 g) peppermint

½ oz (15 g) dried lemon balm

Stir all the ingredients together in a clockwise motion.
You can store this in a tin or colored jar for up to a
year for those special evenings. When you are
ready to brew the tea, pour boiling water over the
herbs, two teaspoons for a cup of water. Say the
following spell aloud during the 5-minute
steeping and picture your heart's desire.

Herbal brew of love's emotion

With my wish I fortify

When two people share this potion

This love shall intensify

As in the Olde Garden of Love.

Sweeten to taste with honey and
share this luscious libation with
the one you love.

BREWING UP A BATCH OF PASSION

For a passionate pick-me-up, drink this tasty tonic with your lover.

GATHER TOGETHER

½ cup (120 ml) lemonade

2 mugs

2 cups (480 ml) freshly drawn water

½ cup (50 g) sliced fresh ginger root

1 teaspoon cardamom

Honey, to sweeten

Pour half of the lemonade into each mug. Boil the ginger and cardamom in the water for 4 minutes, strain, then pour into the mugs and sweeten with honey to taste. Before you drink this lustful libation, simply say:

Gift of the Goddess and magic of moon,

May the flower of our love come to full bloom.

Shared between two lovers before a tryst, this enchanted potion will give great endurance for a memorable encounter. Each sip is full of love's sure power.

LAVENDER- AND ROSEMARY-INFUSED VODKA

Vodka is easily infused with the flavor of flowers, herbs, fruit, and even vegetables. Try this combination of lavender, to calm and heal, and rosemary, to dispel negative spirits.

Both of these are love herbs. What could be better? When you've finished infusing the vodka, tie the dried herbs into a bundle with string and use them when you next make a fire in the hearth. The scented smoke will imbue your home with coziness, calm, healing, and love.

GATHER TOGETHER

2 sprigs fresh rosemary

3 sprigs fresh lavender

1 quart (1 liter) vodka

Rinse the herbs in cool water and gently pat them dry. Put them in a sterilized quart (1 liter) Mason jar, pour in vodka to cover the herbs to the top, and seal tightly. Shake vigorously and place in your pantry or a dark closet, making sure to shake it at least once a day. After two days, take a spoon and taste the vodka. If the taste suits you, go ahead and strain the herbs out using cheesecloth (muslin) or a paper coffee filter. Otherwise leave it another day, up to a maximum of 5 days in total. Set the herbs aside and leave them to dry. Pour the strained vodka into a bottle, and label it with its name and the date. Your infused vodka will taste wonderful served ice-cold and neat. To your health!

STERILIZING YOUR CANNING JARS

Wash the jars in hot soapy water and rinse in scalding water or use a dishwasher on the hottest setting. Place the jars on a rack set in a deep pot and cover with hot water. Bring the water to a boil and boil the canning jars, covered, for 15 minutes. Using jar tongs, carefully remove the jars, empty out any hot water, and sit them upside down on a clean, dry towel. Once dry, they are ready to fill with your potions and produce!

LONGEVITY PEAR ELIXIR

Pears have long been prized in Asia for being a lucky fruit that also offers a long and prosperous life. The great magical teacher Scott Cunningham advocated their use in love spells. This pear liqueur is a special brew indeed.

GATHER TOGETHER

2 cardamom pods

3 large ripe pears

2 in (5 cm) piece of lemon peel

1 quart (1 liter) vodka

Sterilize a 1 quart (1 liter) Mason jar with a lid, preferably a dark-colored one if you can find it. Crush the cardamom pods and set aside. Peel and core the pears and cut into thin slices. Gently place the pears in the jar. Put the  crushed cardamom and lemon peel on top, and cover all with the vodka, leaving a gap of 1 in (2.5 cm) at the top. Close the jar and tighten the lid, then gently shake it twice. Store it in a cool, dark cupboard or closet for 10 days. When the time is up, pour the contents into a mixing bowl and mash thoroughly using the back of a fork or a potato masher. Strain the mixture into another bowl, using a colander lined with a paper coffee filter or cheesecloth (muslin). Repeat this process twice, then pour the pear liqueur back into a sterilized Mason jar. If you're feeling fancy, store the liqueur in a pretty bottle, but make sure it is sterilized and tightly sealed. Live long and prosper!

CHAPTER 5

CURATIVE CONCOCTIONS

WITCHY CURATIVE BREWS

Wellness can and should be easy. It shouldn't stress us out to manage our stress, right? Try making a simple tea using one of the herbs listed.

Keep it simple by using one tablespoon of your chosen herb for every quart (liter) of hot water. Steep for at least 30 minutes, or 45 minutes if you like stronger brews. Strain, then serve or store. Keep notes in your Book of Shadows or self-care journal regarding what works best for you. I am often surprised and still find it thrilling that chicory is a real energy herb for me. When you've found what works, stick with it!

★ **For purifying:** Dandelion greens, lemon balm, or nettle leaves.

★ **For less stress:** Astragalus, dandelion root, or ginseng.

★ **For calm breath:** Ginger root, licorice root, or marshmallow root.

★ **For improved mood:** Ginger root, lemon balm, or rose hips.

★ **For women's wellness:** Ginger root, peppermint, or red raspberry leaf.

★ **For good sleep:** Chamomile, lavender, or thyme.

STRAIN SLAYERS AND TENSION TAMERS

Mother Nature's wisdom is infinite. The good news is that there are lots of wonderful herbs that are strongly effective against anxiety, and they don't share the same risk of addiction and dependence that comes with pharmaceutical anti-anxiety medications, such as benzodiazepines.

Like all medicinals, these herbs and tinctures aren't right for everyone, but they can be tremendously helpful when they're used at the correct dose and are correctly matched to your needs. It's important to remember that herbs aren't like drugs; there's no specific anxiety herb that can be prescribed for you. You are looking for the herb that's the best match for you. Avoid taking any of these herbs (unless otherwise directed by a qualified practitioner) if you're taking prescription medication for sleep, anxiety, or depression.

Tinctures made from natural herbs are gentle and good for you, but I recommend using one at a time for full effect. This way, you will learn something very important—what is most effective for you.

ALLEVIATE ANXIETY
WITH HERBS

Remember, these herbs are helpers on your journey to healing your anxiety. All of your other lifestyle practices, including breath work, exercise, journal writing, a healthy diet, and reaching out for support from friends, family, and practitioners, are still important— but there's no question that life with anxiety is a lot easier with safe and effective herbal remedies in your back pocket.

★ **Kava kava:** This is the most famous anti-anxiety herb, and with good reason. It is more sedating and hypnotic than passionflower and skullcap and has an intriguing taste that almost numbs your mouth. Some people find that it creates a blissed-out feeling. In Polynesia, it has a long tradition of use in rituals as well as in medicines for its sedative and pain-relieving properties. You can try using this herb up to three or four times per week to help relieve your anxiety. It's effective as a tea, as a substitute for skullcap in your tincture recipes, or as store-bought capsules, but tea or tincture are best.

★ **St John's wort:** This is one of the most relied-upon of all herbal treatments for mild to moderate depression, PMS, perimenopause symptoms, and its general immune- and mood-boosting effects. It is so popular now that you can find the extract at most pharmacies, grocers, herbal supply stores, and health-food stores. For brighter days, take 300 to 600 milligrams using a dropper under your tongue so it enters your system safely and swiftly. Most places that sell the extract also sell dropper bottles.

★ **Hibiscus:** Beloved for the heavenly scented perfume of the flowers, hibiscus is also a powerful relaxant and can even lower blood pressure. As if that is not enough, it can help relieve sore throats and colds. As with other herbal applications, steeping a tablespoon of the dried flowers in a cup of freshly boiled water for 10 minutes twice a day produces a healing tea. This sweet-smelling and tasting floral remedy can help you reset and recharge.

SIMPLE SKULLCAP TINCTURE FOR COMFORT AND CALM

This simple and easy recipe using the comforting skullcap herb makes a very fine tincture that has many medicinal uses.

GATHER TOGETHER

¼ cup (15 g) dried skullcap

2 cups (480 ml) apple cider vinegar
or 1 cup (240 ml) vodka and 1 cup (240 ml) water

1 quart (1 liter) canning jar

Cheesecloth (muslin), a 6 in (15 cm) square

6 fl oz (175 ml) colored storage jar that seals

Label and pen

Put the dried skullcap in the canning jar and carefully pour in the vinegar. Stir well and seal. Place on a dark shelf and shake once a day. After a month, strain through cheesecloth or muslin. Compost the herbal residue in your garden and store the tincture in a colored and sealable glass jar. Lastly, label it and I like to add the astrological information along with the phase of the moon.

You may also want to record this in your Book of Shadows—it will be helpful to you and your family to know that tinctures made in the New Taurus Moon, for example, have the most healing power for you, or whichever it turns out to be.

SKULLCAP HERBAL HELPER

Your skullcap tincture will greatly alleviate anxiety and a downward spiral of moods. Even better, it comes in handy as a mouthwash and hair rinse and for ritual baths, and even as a rub for achy joints and sore muscles.

For a cup of skullcap tea, add one teaspoon of the tincture to a cup of hot water, add a teaspoon of honey, stir, and enjoy. Your tincture will keep for a year but you'll probably use it up much sooner! This kind of kitchen witchery always reminds me of how lucky we are for Mother Nature's bounty. Expressing our gratitude to her adds a sacred aspect to this healing work.

All that we have is thanks to you,

Great goddess, who makes the sky blue.

All that we will receive is thanks to you,

Good goddess, we are grateful for all you do.

This we pray with love eternal and boundless gratitude.

REMEDY RECIPES

Many remedies can be made from what you have in the kitchen, from spices as well as herbs and plants. Here are a few simple tried-and-tested recipes handed down through generations of wise women.

★ **Nutmeg milk:** Grated nutmeg soothes heartburn, nausea, and upset tummies. Use a grater to grate a small amount (about ⅛ teaspoon) to 1 mug of warmed milk (cow, soy, rice, or oat milk). It is comforting and curling.

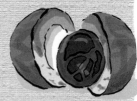

★ **Cayenne infusion:** Use this pepper as a remedy for colds, coughs, sore throats, heartburn, hemorrhoids, and varicose veins, or as a digestive stimulant and to improve circulation. Make an infusion by adding ½ teaspoon cayenne powder to 1 cup (240 ml) boiled water. Add 2 cups (480 ml) of hot water to make a more pleasant and palatable infusion. Add lemon and honey to taste.

⋆ **Catnip by the cup:** This herb is not just for kitties! We humans can also benefit from it as a remedy for upset tummies as well as a way to diminish worry, anxiety, and nervous tension. Take a palmful of dried catnip leaves and steep in a cup (240 ml) of boiling water for 5 minutes. Strain as you would any loose tea. Honey helps even more and a cup or two of catnip tea per day will have you in fine fettle, relaxed and ready.

⋆ **Cranberry cure:** How many times did your mom tell you to drink your cranberry juice? Turns out she was right to insist. Unsweetened cranberry juice is very good for bladder health and also benefits men as it's great for prostate health, too. Two half cups (two lots of 120 ml) a day, mom's orders!

⋆ **Echinacea root:** Every herb store or organic grocer will have dried echinacea root for fighting colds and negating respiratory infections. It is an amazing immune booster! Just mince a teaspoonful and steep in a cup (240 ml) of boiling water. Sweeten to taste and drink at least a couple of cups a day.

OTHER HERBS FOR MEDICINAL TEAS

You can use the basic recipe of steeping a palmful of herbs for
5 minutes in a cup (240 ml) of boiling water and use these plants
either fresh or dried:

★ **Lemon balm** is a true aid for insomnia, anxiety, and restlessness.

★ **Licorice root** is marvelous for stomach and mouth ulcers.

★ **Marshmallow**, both root and leaf, strengthens the gastrointestinal
tract and your mucus membranes.

★ **Milk thistle** is excellent for your liver and kidneys.

★ **Mullein leaves** help sore throats, coughs, and chest congestion.

★ **Nettle**, either fresh or dried, prevents allergies.

★ **Slippery elm bark** will get rid of heartburn, a bad cough, and
a sore throat.

★ **St John's wort** extract is good for depression, PMS,
and hot flashes.

★ **Thyme** is trusted to help with colds and
congestion and is an antispasmodic.

LAVENDER AND CHAMOMILE TRANQUILITY TONIC

In the hurly burly of work weeks and packed calendars, we often find ourselves feeling drained and a bit down in the dumps. When we are fatigued, feelings of gloom can arise.

At my house we say "a tonic in time saves nine" because this herbal healer can fend off the bad feelings and perk you right up. Herbal tonics, which are concentrated reductions of the herbs, last longer and provide a higher dose of the herb than teas or tisanes.

GATHER TOGETHER

1½ cups (80 g) dried lavender

1½ cups (80 g) dried chamomile

1 cup (240 ml) clear alcohol, such as vodka

2 cups (480 ml) distilled water

Clear quart (liter) jar with lid

Cheesecloth (muslin), a 6 in (15 cm) square

Dark glass storage jar with lid

Place the dried herbs into your clear jar. Pour in the alcohol. Add in the distilled water, put on the lid securely, and shake for a few minutes until it seems well mixed. Store in a dark cupboard for 30 days, shaking once a day.

Then strain through the cheesecloth or muslin into the storage jar and screw the lid on tightly. The lavender and chamomile leavings will make lovely compost for your witch's garden and the liquid tonic will soon prove itself indispensable in your household.

EASY APPLE CIDER VINEGAR

This easy-peasy recipe will result in one of the most useful items in your pantry that can be used in your cookery, as a daily health drink, household cleanser, skin, and facial toner, a hair rinse, and dozens of other excellent applications.

Hippocrates, the founding father of Western medicine in ancient Greece, taught that he depended on two medicinal tonics, honey and vinegar. Apple cider vinegar lowers cholesterol and blood pressure and helps strengthen bones; best of all, it costs mere pennies to make as you are only using the cores and peels from the apples. Bake a couple of pies while you brew up a tonic health booster. When you add herbs to vinegar, you are enhancing the healing power of the best of both worlds.

GATHER TOGETHER

8 organic apple cores and peels

1 quart (1 liter) water

2 tablespoons honey

Cut up the apple cores and peels into smaller pieces and spoon into a wide-mouthed canning jar. Cover the fruit in water, spoon in the honey, and stir well.

Cover the mixture with a paper towel or waxed paper and place a rubber band tightly around the neck of the jar. Place on a dark shelf and leave for two weeks. Strain the liquid and remove the solids that remain, return the liquid to the jar, and secure the band again. Put it back on the shelf and make sure to stir daily. After one month, take a spoonful and if the acidity and flavor is to your taste, transfer to a dark bottle with sealable top. If not, wait another week, then taste it again. Vinegar will corrode metal lids so a bottle with a cork is the best option.

HERBAL ALCHEMY

The leaves and stalks of these plants are very good for making herbal vinegars: apple mint, basil, catnip, garlic mustard, orange mint, peppermint, rosemary, spearmint, thyme, and yarrow. Roots also infuse nicely into herbal vinegars—the best are dandelion, chicory, ginger, garlic, mugwort, and burdock.

OXYMEL: AN ANCIENT TONIC

Oxymel is a very old-fashioned tonic that dates back to ancient times but has fallen out of fashion. It remains a favorite of herbal healers and is made of two seemingly opposing ingredients—honey and vinegar.

Oxymels are supremely effective for respiratory issues. The recipe is simplicity itself, equal parts honey and vinegar poured over herbs in a canning jar. Store in a dark cupboard and give the sealed jar a good shake every day. After two weeks, strain out the herbs through cheesecloth (muslin) and store in the fridge.

HERBS FOR OXYMELS

The herbs that I would recommend using for this healing tonic are oregano, elderflower, sage, lemon balm, mint, lemon peel, thyme, lavender, rose petals, hyssop, and fennel.

BLACKBERRIES: ROADSIDE MEDICINE

Blackberries are one of life's sweetest gifts, growing abundantly in the bramble along many a rambling path.

An extremely effective medicinal tonic can be made by soaking 4 cups (520 g) of berries in a quart (1 liter) of malt vinegar for three days. Drain and strain the liquid into a pan. Simmer and stir in sugar, 2¼ cups (450 g) to every 2 cups (480 ml) of tonic. Boil gently for 5 minutes and skim off any foam. Cool and pour into a sealable jar.

This potion is so powerful that you can add a teaspoon into a cup of water and cure tummy aches, cramps, fevers, coughs, and colds. Best of all, blackberry vinegar is both a medicine and a highly prized culinary flavoring for sauces and salads. Pour some over your apple pie and cream and you will soon scurry off to pick blackberries all summer.

FLOWER ESSENCE GENTLE REMEDY

I am happy to share my family recipe, lovingly handed down through several generations. To make your own flower essences at home, start by making a mother tincture—the most concentrated form of the essence—which can then be used to make stock bottles. The stock bottles are used to make dosage bottles for the most diluted form of the essence, which is the one you actually take.

GATHER TOGETHER

Handful of freshly picked flowers specific to the malady being treated

6 pints (2.8 liters) fresh pure water or distilled water

Organic brandy or vodka, at least 40 percent proof

Large glass mixing bowl

Tweezers or chopsticks

Cheesecloth (muslin)

Large pitcher (jug)

Green or blue sealable glass bottles

Ideally, begin early in the morning, picking your chosen flowers (all of the same species) by 9 a.m. at the latest. This leaves you with three hours of sunlight before the noon hour, after which the sunlight is less effective, even draining.

Put the water in a large glass mixing bowl. To avoid touching the flowers, use tweezers or chopsticks to place them carefully on the surface of the water, until the surface is covered. Leave the bowl in the sun for three to four hours, or until the flowers begin to fade.

Now, delicately remove the flowers, being careful not to touch the water. Strain the flower essence water through cheesecloth into a large pitcher (jug). Half-fill a green or blue 8 fl oz (225 ml) sealable glass bottle with the flower essence water and top up with the brandy or vodka (this will extend the shelf life of your flower water to three months if stored in a cool, dark cupboard).

This is your mother tincture. Label it with the date and the name of the flower. Use any remaining essence water to water the flowers you've been working with and murmur a prayer of gratitude for their healing power.

To make a stock bottle from your mother tincture, fill a 1 fl oz (30 ml) dropper bottle three quarters full of brandy, top up with spring water, then add three drops of the mother tincture. This will last at least three months and enable you to make lots of dosage bottles.

To make a dosage bottle for any flower essence, just add two or three drops from the stock bottle to another 1 fl oz (30 ml) dropper bottle one quarter full of brandy and three quarters full of distilled water. Any time you need some of this gentle medicine, place four drops from the dosage bottle under your tongue or add it to a glass of water. Take or sip four times a day, or as often as you feel the need. You can't overdose on flower remedies, but more frequent, rather than larger, doses are much more effective.

A FLORAL HEALER FOR
EACH SIGN OF THE ZODIAC

Some of the most blessed of brews are custom designed for us by Mother Nature herself using the wisdom of the sun, moon, and stars. Floral waters and flower essences express emotional benefits differently and each has special healing applications.

As we can tell from the mass popularity of Bach's Rescue Remedy, they work wonderfully to abet emotional health, mental outlook, and positivity. The specifics of these curatives can be pretty direct. For example, the flower impatiens helps those who struggle with impatience. Magical, right? I recommend sticking with the recommended dosage of three to four drops taken via the bottle dropper.

Aries—impatiens renewal for rams: High-energy Arians race forward, blazing new trails. Patience is not their strong suit. When the going gets tough, rams just hurry on, never stopping, which can be a major source of undue stress and strain. Try impatiens flower essence and you'll discover a wellspring of fortitude.

Taurus—chestnut-bud benefits for bulls: Security-loving Taureans prefer safe harbor and no surprises, but a life of routine can lead to feelings of being stuck in a rut and sameness. Freshen up your day to day with chestnut bud.

Gemini—madia mental magic for twins: Curious Geminis are liable to overwork their brains to the point of over-thinking. Preserve your intellectual power with a mental boost. Madia may be a great flower essence to try because it's said to calm the waves of a wandering mind.

Cancer—honeysuckle health for crabs: Cancerians have a legendary love of history, so much so that they can start living there. Resist the pull of the past with sweet honeysuckle essence.

Leo—borage for brave lions: Loving, giving, and so dramatic, Leos leave nothing behind as they live life at full tilt, which can be emotionally exhausting and lead to many a heartbreak. When this happens, anyone, especially Leos, should turn to borage flower essence. Borage offers encouragement and can move you from sadness and hurt to healing and openheartedness.

Virgo—pine helps perfectionists: Sticklers by nature, Virgos work hard to be organized, on time, and have things just so, but none of us is perfect so that can be a setup for failure. Falling short of your own extremely high standards can lead to a swirl of condemnatory self-talk and a cycle of negativity. Reconnect to self-compassion with pine essence.

Libra—scleranthus serenity: Librans are often caught in a balancing act of weighing, and reweighing, their options before making a decision, which can lead to vacillation and hesitancy. To spur determination, try scleranthus flower essence, which encourages clear thinking and real balance.

Scorpio—holly is holy: Scorpios are the tops for intensity and passions, which can lead to heartache, disappointment, upset, and even anger. Evergreen holly helps you to feel the universe's eternal love and brings balance to your life. If you feel like you are bumping up against endless frustration, tap into holly's holy life-giving energy.

Sagittarius—vervain gives vivacity: Energizer bunnies describes Sagittarians. While sharing their ideals with others fuels their joie de vivre spirit, such ardent enthusiasm can sometimes lead to setting overly optimistic goals. If you need support in balancing impassioned pursuits with a pragmatic perspective, try vervain flower essence.

Capricorn—oak prevents overwhelm: Unbelievably strong, these loveable goats may never stop, which can lead to burnout. Capricorns try to do everything on their own, drawing too much on their own can-do spirit, which can be a grueling path to achieving goals. Oak is a marvelous flower essence for helping to set boundaries, energy preservation, and maintaining rather than draining yourself while you get to the top of that mountain.

 Aquarius—California wild rose reduces pain and fever, boosts immunity and mood: Water bearers are individuals, forging their own path, and all that freethinking can create distance between themselves and others. Aquarians can become too detached from people, even loved ones, and can also separate from the practicality of their own life. When you feel the gaps growing, turn to California wild rose, which will re-energize your sense of purpose and your ties to the important things in life.

Pisces—pink yarrow soothes both jangled nerves and the stomach: Pisceans are deeply empathetic to the point of being psychic and the big issue can be boundaries. Too much taking on of other people's feelings can cause emotional muddles, sadness, depression, anxiety, and overwhelm. Sensitivity and compassion are beautiful as long as you can draw and maintain clear boundaries between yourself and others. Pink yarrow helps you to maintain mental clarity, good self-esteem, and healthy relationships.

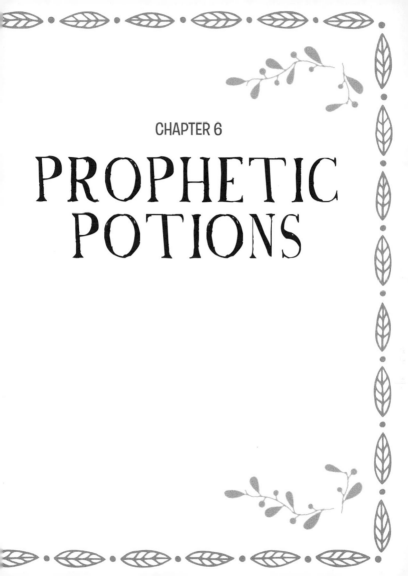

CHAPTER 6

PROPHETIC POTIONS

POTION OF PLENTY

The humble dandelion, considered a bothersome weed by some, hides its might well. Dandelion root tea can help you find lost treasure, money, wallets, even people. When you drink it in direct moonlight, sleep will be sweet, and clues and messages will appear in your dreams.

GATHER TOGETHER

Mortar and pestle

2 tablespoons dried dandelion root

2 cups (480 ml) freshly boiled water

Teapot

Oven mitts

Large heat-resistant bowl

Strainer

With your mortar and pestle, grind the dandelion root and steep in the freshly boiled water in your teapot. Pour into the bowl through the strainer. Now slip on your oven mitts and hold the bowl in your hands. Say aloud seven times what you are looking for. Afterward, pour the potion onto your front stoop or the steps in front of your home. What you are looking for will return to you.

TELEPATHY TEA

Dandelion root tea can also call upon the spirit of anyone whose advice you might need.

Simply place a freshly brewed simple (see page 11) using this herbal root on your bedroom altar or nightstand. Before you sleep, say the name of your helper aloud seven times. In a dream or vision, the spirit will visit you and answer all your questions. During medieval times, this spell was used to find hidden treasure. Chaucer, who was well-versed in astrology and other metaphysics, advised this tried-and-true tea.

BINDING LOVE POTION

When we are in love, we all hope for it to be requited. Spellcraft can help with that! Here's one to share with your lover.

GATHER TOGETHER

2 teaspoons dried lemon balm, basil, blackberry, or magnolia buds

2 cups (480 ml) water

Teapot and 2 mugs

Honey, to sweeten

Boil the water and add to the teapot along with the herbs. Steep for 3 minutes, then pour into the mugs and sweeten. Intone this spell as you stir:

Lover be faithful, lover be true.

This is all I am asking of you.

Give thy heart to nobody but me.

This is my will.

So mote it be.

Before you and your lover share this special treat together, whisper this wish in secret:

Honey magnolia [or whichever herb you chose],
Goddess's herb.

Perform for me enchantment superb.

Let _____ [name of lover] and I be as one.

As ever, harm to none.

This spell must be sealed with a kiss between you and your beloved. Now enjoy drinking the tea with the object of your affection, from whom you wish not to stray, and his or her loyalty will never sway.

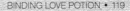

SPICE UP YOUR LIFE SPELL

Start a fresh chapter in your love life without delay with this cup of love.

GATHER TOGETHER

Cinnamon spice tea (from a store) or 3 chopped cinnamon sticks

1 cup (240 ml) hot water

1 teaspoon honey

1 teaspoon ground cinnamon (or 3 more sticks ground in your mortar and pestle)

Brew and steep the tea for at least 3 minutes. Stir in the honey and savor the sweet, spicy smell. Drink it while contemplating your hopes, intentions, and dreams for a happy, healthy love life. Now, sprinkle the ground version of this charismatic spice on the threshold of your front door and along your entry path. When the cinnamon powder is crushed underfoot, its regenerative powers will help heat things up in your love life.

LUCK BY THE CUP

When you are crafting money magic, it is good to get into the manifesting mindset with some prosperity tea.

GATHER TOGETHER

1 tablespoon dried rose hips

1 tablespoon dried chamomile

1 teaspoon orange peel

2 cups (480 ml) freshly boiled water

Teapot

Green mug

Strainer

1 cinnamon stick

Steep the rose hips, chamomile, and orange peel in the freshly boiled water in the teapot for 4 minutes. Pour the tea into the mug through the strainer, and stir widdershins, or counterclockwise, with the cinnamon stick for a moment. As you drink, visualize the abundance coming into your life in your household.

GHOSTBUSTING POTION

To rid a house of haunting intrusion, brew a peppermint-and-clove infusion.

Draw fresh water and boil it in your teakettle. Place three cloves in the bottom of a teacup and add either a peppermint teabag or a handful of fresh mint leaves from your herb pots. Pour hot water into the cup and let it steep for 10 minutes, then let cool. Dip your fingers in the cup and sprinkle the potion throughout the space, and out, out, the ghost will race. Burning frankincense and myrrh incense sends negative spirits flying away, as well. This ritual is best done during a waning moon.

MUGWORT FOR
MYSTICAL VISIONS

Mugwort has long been regarded as an herb sacred to the Triple Goddess, cronehood, and the moon because it is so powerful. It is a divinatory herb and can be used to bring out psychism and invoke visionary states inducing astral travel.

Mugwort beer was a favorite in medieval times. It is also a protector herb and, unsurprisingly, can be used to ward off psychic attacks and curses. Many witches sleep with mugwort under their pillow for the protection it provides.

By steeping mugwort in hot water, you can make a tonic that offers great calm and is also soothing to the stomach. As an essential oil, it can be rubbed on front doors, windows, your altar, and anywhere you feel the need to be safer and secure. It can also safeguard against injury and preserve your personal strength and vitality.

Mugwort plants can also be bundled, dried and bound together for a broom specially used to sweep any bad energy from your home. Leaves can be dried and used like sage for smudging. Mugwort wreaths hung on the front door will prevent negative energy from entering your home.

DANDELION
DIVINATION WINE

One woman's weed is another's prized secret for myriad mystical uses—delectable sautéed greens and mixed salads and therapeutic teas as well as a very special kind of wine.

Hedge witches have known for centuries that this hardy specimen can be used for calling upon helpful spirits, dispelling negative energy, and bringing good luck. One of the most important uses of this herb is divination, making this wine an absolutely enchanting way to foresee the future.

GATHER TOGETHER

14 oz (400 g) freshly picked and cleaned dandelion blossoms (no stems or leaves)

1 orange and 1 lemon, thinly sliced

1 gallon (3.8 liters) freshly boiled water

6¾ cups (1.35 kg) organic sugar

1 piece of dried bread

½ oz (15 g) dry yeast

IN VINO VERITAS: VISIONARY WINE

Marigolds are said to lend prophetic powers and more; you can make a wine using the exact same recipe as for dandelion wine, but make sure to pick the marigolds when the flowers have fully opened by the light of the sun. Drink the marigold wine when you desire to have prophetic visions and record them. Celebrate and commemorate these dreams and visions as vital information could come as a result—after all, in wine, truth.

Place the flowers in a very large bowl that can handle heat; place the orange and lemon slices on top of the flowers and pour in the hot water. Cover the bowl with a clean, dry towel and place on a pantry shelf for ten days. Strain the mixture into a different bowl and spoon in the sugar, stirring to dissolve. Toast the bread and spread the yeast on top, then let it float on top of your mixture. Cover and let sit for another three days. Strain the liquid and compost the bread and any flower remains. Bottle your dandelion wine in special bottles, cork, and label it. This is a marvelous libation to share during Wiccan holidays and anytime you are in need of a positive portent.

PROPHECY POTION

If you and your circle, coven, or group want to increase your abilities to intuit and invent together, brew up a batch of creative juices at a Wednesday gathering.

GATHER TOGETHER

½ cup (30 g) of dried herbs: kava kava, borage, mugwort, yarrow, or dandelion

4 cups (960 ml) freshly boiled water

Large teapot and 4 mugs

Steep the herbs in the freshly boiled water in your teapot for 4 minutes, then pour the tea into the four mugs. Before your group begins drinking, say:

Goddess of the Oracles, please give us the sight!

God of the Prophets, please give us the vision!

Fate of the Future, we call on you for truth.

Harm to none, so mote it be.

Notice I did not mention to strain the herbs. In addition to the dreams, visions, and all you will soon foretell, you can begin with these cups of aromatic herbs and read the tea leaves by interpreting the shapes you see at the bottom of the mug once you have drunk the liquid.

★ **An apple** symbolizes knowledge or success in studies.

★ **A candle** indicates wisdom and enlightenment.

★ **A cat** can mean you have a deceitful friend.

★ **A dog** can mean you have someone loyal in your life.

★ **Flying birds** represent a letter bearing a happy message.

★ **Ravens** are an omen of troubles ahead.

★ **A shamrock** shows a wish will come true.

★ **Kite** shapes show good news flying to you.

★ **A letter** of the alphabet references a person whose name starts with that letter.

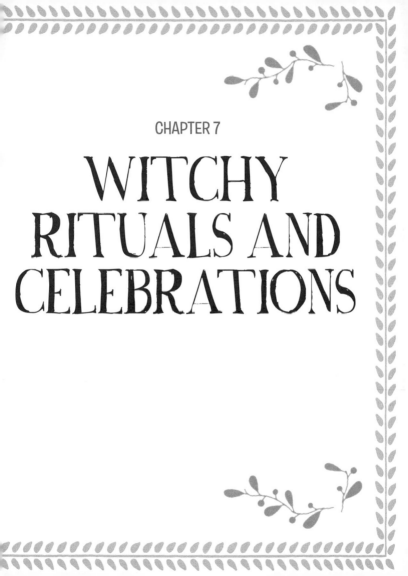

CHAPTER 7

WITCHY RITUALS AND CELEBRATIONS

CLEARING CLUTTER

Before you can do any ritual work, you must clear the clutter that can create blocks. Banish old, bad energy by following this spell.

First, make an energy-clearing lavender-and-mint tea by drawing fresh water, boiling it, and adding 4 sprigs each of fresh lavender and fresh mint (if you have no access to the fresh herbs, use 1 teaspoon of each dried herb instead). Steep for at least 4 minutes, and as long as 10 minutes if there is a lot of energetic clutter. Leave it to cool, then dip your finger in the tea and sprinkle it throughout your home while reciting:

Clean and clear, nothing negative near.

Only healing and helpful energies here.

With harm to none. So mote it be.

Repeat three times, and if you feel the need to clear out any remaining cloud of psychic clutter, add the diluted tea to your cleaner when you wash floors or surfaces. The scent of calm and clarity will lift the spirits of all who enter your space.

HEART'S EASE CAULDRON CURE

Here is a soothing sip that can uplift your spirits while also warding off chills. This combination of herbs brings about the "letting go" of sorrows, worries, and doubts, and reignites feelings of self-love.

GATHER TOGETHER

1 oz (25 g) dried rose hips

1 oz (25 g) dried hibiscus

2 oz (50 g) dried mint

1 tablespoon dried ginger root

Stir all the ingredients together in a cauldron. Pour into a colored jar and seal. When you are ready to brew, pour hot water over the herbs, two teaspoons per cup. While this steeps for 5 minutes, write down any thoughts or fears of which you need to rid yourself. Say each one aloud, then chant, "Begone!" After this letting-go ritual, burn the paper together with sage in the cauldron on your altar. As you sip the tea, enjoy your renewed sense of self and peace of mind.

YIN AND YANG RITE

Did you know that three cups of herbal tea each day not only offers you tranquility but also a marvelous boost to heart and liver health, as well as better sleep and moods?

Simply put, drinking a big pot of tea each day is one of the easiest and best things you can do for yourself. Therefore, I suggest dedicating a sacred space to this rite you should observe often. The gift this tea brings us is that of fire and water, combining the energies of yang and yin.

GATHER TOGETHER

3 comfy and colorful pillows

Small low table

Single orchid

Japanese incense, such as plum blossom or jasmine

Fireproof dish or incense burner

Large ceramic teapot and cup

Japanese green tea

Find the most comfortable place in your home and place the pillows on the floor. Set up the low table for taking tea each day and establish a peaceful environment with no clutter. Place the orchid and incense on the table—a light and clean scented Japanese incense is the perfect energetic balancer and cleanser.

Steep some freshly brewed tea in your big pot and set it on the small table beside the flower. Light the incense, place it in the burner, and settle back on the pillows. Sit for three minutes with your eyes closed, breathing in the lightly floral scent of the incense. Clear your mind; think of nothing outside of this moment.

Taking tea in this ritualized style helps keep everything in balance for you—it allows you to escape the material world for a time, and then return, refreshed and rebalanced.

CAKES AND ALE: SATURN-DAY NIGHT FEVER

Here is a pagan party plan, which is wonderful for weekend evenings. You can add many embellishments, such as important astrological or lunar happenings, but you should gather your friends or coven and celebrate life any Saturday night of your choosing.

If the weather is warm enough, have the festivities outside. Otherwise, make sure to choose an indoor space with enough room for dancing, drumming, and major merriment. Ask each of your guests to bring cake, cookies, and candies of their choice along with their favorite beer, wine, mead, cider, or ale, and sitting cushions. Place the offerings on a center-table altar and light candles of all colors. Once everyone is seated and settled, the host or designated circle leader chants:

Gods of Nature, bless these cakes,

That we may never suffer hunger.

Goddess of the harvest,

Bless this ale,

That we may never suffer thirst. Blessed be.

The eldest and the youngest should serve the food and drink to all in the circle. Lastly, they serve each other and the leader chants the blessing again. Let the feasting begin!

BELTANE BREW

Beltane, celebrated on April 30, is without doubt the sexiest of pagan high holidays, and it is anticipated greatly throughout the year. Witchy ones celebrate this holy night, and it is traditional for celebrations to last all through the night.

This is a festival for feasting, singing, laughter, and lovemaking. On May Day, when the sun returns in the morning, revelers gather to erect a merrily beribboned Maypole to dance around, followed by picnics and sensual siestas. The following recipe is befitting this special time of the year when love flows as freely as wine.

Honeyed mead is revered as the drink of choice for this sexiest of pagan holy days. It is an aphrodisiac and signals the ripeness of this day devoted to love and lust. This recipe is adapted from a medieval method.

GATHER TOGETHER

1 quart (1 liter) honey

3 quarts (3 liters) distilled water

Herbs to flavor, such as cinnamon, nutmeg, or vanilla, according to your preference

1 packet (7 g) of active dry yeast

Mix the honey and water. Boil for 5 minutes. You can add the herbs to your liking but I prefer a tablespoon each of clove, nutmeg, cinnamon, and allspice. Add a packet of yeast and mix. Put everything in a large container. Cover with plastic wrap and allow to rise and expand. Store the mix in a dark place and allow it to set for seven days, ideally at the beginning of a new moon phase. Refrigerate for three days while the sediment settles at the bottom. Strain and store in a colored glass bottle, preferably green. You can drink it now but after seven months, it will have gained a full-bodied flavor. Always keep it in a cool dark place.

MIDSUMMER'S DAY DREAM TEA COOLER

Not every herbal tea will work over ice, but this one will have your family and friends clamoring for more.

GATHER TOGETHER

1 part each of lemon verbena, lemon balm, mint, chamomile, and hibiscus

2 cups (480 ml) peach juice

1 lemon

Gather a handful of the dried herbs. Place them in a pot, pour over 6 cups (1.5 liters) of boiling water, and let cool to room temperature. Pour into a large pitcher and add the peach juice to two-thirds full. Give a good stir and add in enough ice cubes to fill the container. Slice the lemon and lay it on top. Serve, sit back, and let the compliments begin. This convivial concoction is ideal for special summer occasions, such as the midsummer celebration of the solstice.

PRAYER TO HONOR
THE SUMMER

For summer festivals, such as the Summer Solstice on June 21,
you should honor the deities who gift us with such plenty.
Light yellow and green candles at your altar and on the feast
table and offer this appeal:

Oh, Lady of Summer

Who brings sun and life-giving rains,

May each harvest bring the crops
that fill our cups,

The rivers and oceans, fields and farms
are yours.

We honor you today and give thanks to you
for all we have.

A toast to thee, blessed be!

HOT CIDER

For any high holiday or sabbat festival, this is a blessed brew that will not only create conviviality but also imbue your home with a heaven-sent fragrance.

GATHER TOGETHER

1 gallon (4.5 liters) apple cider

Large stockpot

Peel of half an orange, cut into pieces

1 heaping teaspoon fresh ginger root, diced

2 star anise pods

3 cinnamon sticks, cut in half

1 tablespoon whole cloves

Small muslin bag and string to tie

Pour the cider into the pot and place on a low heat. Put the orange peel and the spices into the muslin bag and tie with a string. Now add the spice bundle into the pot and let simmer to a slow boil. Once the brew has reached a rolling boil, turn off the heat and serve delightful and delicious mugs full of magic.

PRAYER TO POMONA

We should always express gratitude to the deities who come to our aid. My guardian goddess, Pomona, is the goddess of orchards and apples and a protector of women. She can be your protector, too. Speak the following words after your daily dose of apple cider vinegar or after sipping a cup of hot cider:

She of sylvan hills who watches over,

Keep us safe, keep us whole.

Accept this prayer of thanks

For your abundant wisdom

And generosity in gratitude eternal.

INDEX